Thirty Days to Overcoming:

Meditations for the Way Forward

By the Rev. Louis V. Alexander

Searchlight Press
Dallas, Texas

Thirty Days to Overcoming:
Meditations for the Way Forward

By the Rev. Louis V. Alexander

©2012
All Rights Reserved

ISBN: 978-1-936497-13-3

Scripture taken from the
Authorized (King James) Version
(KJV)

Searchlight Press
Who are you looking for?
Publishers of thoughtful Christian books since 1994.
5634 Ledgestone Drive
Dallas, TX 75214-2026
888.896.6081
info@Searchlight-Press.com
www.Searchlight-Press.com

Manufactured in the United States of America

To my father,
L Z Alexander

Texts of Comfort

When I am Weak
Isaiah 40:28-31
Psalms 121

When I am in Need
Psalms 23
Psalms 24

When I am Persecuted
Psalms 140

When I am Tempted
Psalms 141:1-5
Proverbs 3:5-6

When I am Depressed
John 14:1-3
Psalms 27:1

Day 1

Genesis 1:1: *In the beginning God created the heavens and the earth.*

The Eternal God is always first. He is the creator of all things, and by Him all things are sustained. God has no beginning and no ending. He existed before there was a 'when' or a 'where.' He was God in the dateless past, and He will be God in the future. He is ageless. He is never weary, and He never slumbers or sleeps.

Life is never too complicated when we make Him first. He deserves to be first because of who He is and what He has done. God should be first when we wake up every morning. Let our waking prayer be to give Him thanks and seek His direction for the new day. Let us ask His blessings upon all that we endeavor to do.

We need God to be first in all our decisions, that they might be a blessing to others as well as us – and that He be glorified in all that we do. Each day we live for Him, as Acts 17:28 says: *"For in Him we live, and move, and have our being."*

Life, living, is all about God, the creator of all things. He alone is worthy of our praise.

Prayer: Our Father, I humbly bow to you because of who you are and what you have done. To you be glory forever, and praise this day. Amen.

𝔇𝔞𝔶 2

Genesis 1:2-5: *And the earth was without form, and void; and darkness was upon the face of the deep. And the Spirit of God moved upon the face of the waters. And God said, let there be light: and there was light. And God saw the light, that it was good: and God divided the light from darkness. And God called the light day, and the darkness He called night. And the evening and the morning were the first day.*

Chaos, waste, barren, and empty – all are accurate descriptions of what the earth was before God spoke. Here we see the power and divine knowledge of God. He is working with nothing – emptiness and darkness – yet He speaks light into existence. Light means life. Light means knowledge. Light is a sure sign that divinity is involved.

We ourselves have witnessed the first day of creation by His Word. Every day is a gift from God. Every day God is worthy of praise. Every day He is to be first on our agenda.

When we let God be first, life is less complicated. He makes the rough places smooth. He brings the high ways down. He is first because He is our God, our Creator, and Sustainer.

Proverbs. 3:5-6 says, *"Trust in the Lord with all your heart, and lean not on your own understanding; in all your ways acknowledge Him, and He shall direct your path."*

Who knows the next moment, the next hour, and tomorrow – even the next year – better than God?

Prayer: O Lord, I thank you for revealing yourself in creation and in my life. All power is Thine and Thine alone. Amen

𝔇𝔞𝔶 3

Exodus 3:9-10: *Now therefore, behold, the cry of the children of Israel is come unto me, and I have also seen the oppression wherewith the Egyptians oppress them. Come now therefore, and I will send thee unto Pharaoh, that thou mayest bring forth my people the children of Israel out of Egypt.*

God is amazing. He can see and hear, and He is able to change circumstances. He is a living God, and He is concerned about His people. He knows who you are, and He is aware of what you are going through. God's desire is to make life better for all. To do that, though, he needs to bring you out of Egypt (a place of bondage).

Notice our amazing God. He sends leaders of His own choosing, leaders who hear His voice and follow His direction. He sends leaders whom He equips for particular missions at particular times.

He may not have called you to lead, but He has saved you and brought you out of the bondage of sin for a purpose. Ask Him to reveal His purpose to you! Knowing your purpose will give your life new meaning.

When you were born, God had a purpose in mind for your life. It is no accident that you are on planet Earth.

Prayer: Father God, today I will listen for direction. Speak to my heart, that I may know your plans for my life, and help me to say yes to your will! Amen

𝔇𝔞𝔶 4

Exodus 3:13-14: *And Moses said unto God, behold, when I come unto the children, and shall say unto them, the God of your fathers hath sent me unto you; and they shall say to me, what is His name? What shall I say unto them? And God said unto Moses, I AM THAT I AM: and He said, thus shalt thou say unto the children of Israel, I AM hath sent me unto you.*

God's name tells much about Him: "I AM that I AM." This name refers to God as the Self-Existing One. "I AM that I AM," was a revelation of the Eternal Creator and Consummator of redemption – "He who was, is, and shall be." His name means, "I WAS WHO I WAS," "I AM WHO I AM" and "I SHALL BE WHO I SHALL BE."

God is a redeemer physically as well as spiritually. He is able to save the whole man. He is able to meet all of man's needs. Time is not an enemy to God. He does not age along with us. He was, He is, and He shall be.

You can depend on God. He won't let you down.

He's never late, and He never grows weary. We must not attempt to humanize God. We cannot explain Him away entirely – if we could, He wouldn't be God! Yet we know Him by what He reveals to us through His word, His Son, and the Holy Spirit.

Here is the one great consolation in knowing Him – nothing is too hard for God.

Prayer: Father God, today too I will listen for direction. Speak to my heart, that I might know your plans for my life, and help me to say yes to your will! Amen

𝔇𝔞𝔶 5

Psalms 1:1-3: *Blessed is the man that walketh not in the counsel of the ungodly, nor standeth in the way of sinners, nor sitteth in the seat of the scornful. But his delight is in the law of the Lord; and in His law doth he mediate day and night, and he shall be like a tree planted by the rivers of water, that bringeth forth his fruit in his season; his leaf also shall not wither; and whatsoever he doeth shall prosper.*

Verse one describes what a happy life is – a life uninfluenced by sinners, by their words and by their actions. Casual association with the ungodly can be devastating to the Christian, if we are not sharing Christ.

We are compelled to share Christ with the unsaved. It is our duty, and to fail to do so is to fail the One who died for our sins. To fail to share Christ's saving grace is to fail the One who saved us. "Blessed" means happy, and happiness is the product of righteous living.

Verse two tells us how the righteous man occupies his time. He is influenced by the word of God. The happy man finds his identity in the word of God . He finds a sense of direction, and he learns to worship. The God of heaven and earth will bless his life – *"But his delight is the law of the Lord, and in His law he meditates day and night."* Life's every need is in the word of God.

Verse three tells us such a man is blessed. He has life, and there is productivity in his life. *"He shall be like a tree planted by the rivers of waters, that brings forth its fruit in its season, whose leaf also shall not wither; and whatever he does shall prosper."* He is productive in God's season, for he is an evergreen.

Prayer: O God, my creator, my sustainer, Father of the redeemed, teach me how to live before you and my fellow man. Only then will I know true happiness. Amen

𝕯𝖆𝖞 6

Psalms 119:1-3: *Blessed are the undefiled in the way, who walk in the law of the Lord. Blessed are they that keep His testimonies, and that seek Him with the whole heart. They also do no iniquity: they walk in His ways.*

The Psalmist explains that blessing grows out of righteous living. God will bless us as our lifestyle conforms to His word. Our living must be directed by His word. From His word, we learn to obey His law completely. Psalm 119:11 says, *"Thy word have I hid in my heart, that I might not sin against thee."*

Our concern should always be, 'What does the word of God say about this situation?' Since it is true that He is concerned about humankind, we ought to concern ourselves about His word. Psalm 119:105 says, *"Thy word is a lamp unto my feet, and a light unto my path."*

God's word is a light to direct us. Without His word, we are lost and confused. It would be wise to request Him to, *"Order my steps in thy word: and let not any iniquity have dominion over me."*

Control my life! Your way is the only way. As John 14:6 says, *"I am the way, the truth, and the life: no man cometh unto the Father, but by me."*

Prayer: O Eternal Father, teach me how to live for you through your Word. Let me not assume what is acceptable, what is right, what is honest, what is honorable – apart from your Word. Let your Word direct my life. Amen

𝔇𝔞𝔶 7

Isaiah 53:3-5: *He is despised and rejected of men; A man of sorrow, and acquainted with grief: and we hid as it were our faces from Him; He was despised, and we esteemed Him not. Surely He has borne our grief, and carried our sorrows: yet we did esteem Him stricken, smitten of God, and afflicted. But He was wounded for our transgressions, He was bruised for our iniquities: the chastisement of our peace was upon Him; and with His stripes we are healed.*

More than six hundred years before the birth of Jesus Christ, Isaiah wrote about Christ's rejection and suffering. Much of the nation of Israel rejected Him. So many saw nothing about Him that they cared for. So many heard nothing from Him that they deemed important. John 1:11 says, *"He came unto His own, and His own received Him not."*

Is that true of us too? What do you think of Jesus Christ? Do you accept Him as Savior and Lord of your life?

To reject Him is to live as though He does not exist. It is to live as though He has not made provision for your soul. To reject Jesus Christ is to turn a deaf ear to His word.

Israel will realize one day that He died for our sins (Jews and Gentiles), and was raised for our justification. Today, right now, at this moment, Jesus Christ is able to heal us physically. Even more than that, by His finished work at Calvary He can heal our sin-sick souls. Ephesians 2:8 says, *"For by grace are ye saved through faith; and that not of yourselves: it is the gift of God."*

Grace is provided, yet faith must be applied. Romans 10:17 says, *"So then faith cometh by hearing, and hearing by the word of God."*

Prayer: Our Father which art in heaven, thank you for salvation. Thank you that you did not let me die in sin. Strengthen me to share your saving grace today with others who do not know you as Savior. Amen

𝔇𝔞𝔶 8

Matthew 16:13-16: *When Jesus came into the coast of Caesarea Philippi, He asked His disciples, saying, whom do men say that I the Son of man am? And they said, some say that thou art John the Baptist; some Elias; and others Jeremias, or one of the prophets. He said unto them, but whom say ye that I am? And Simon Peter answered and said, thou art the Christ, the Son of the living God.*

Eternal life is predicated on the correct answer to Christ's question: *"Whom do men say that I the Son of man am?"* We may have high thoughts, but by themselves they are never high enough.   Man has always been in need of help to recognize who Jesus Christ is.

So often, we are too blind to see Him. Our minds are too dull to recognize Him. Sin left us in need of help. God the Father, the Son, and the Holy Spirit must bring us into the knowledge of Jesus the Christ. Perhaps He is doing that for you right now, through these words.

When an unbeliever cannot answer this great

question, we who know Him must be as quick and as sure as Simon Peter. Jesus said unto His disciples, *"But whom say ye that I am?"* And Simon Peter answered, *"Thou art the Christ, the Son of the living God."* Jesus Christ is the Anointed One, Son of the only source of life for all that lives – the living God.

Will you accept Jesus Christ today for who He is? If you know Him as Savior and Lord, share the good news with the lost! He is in the saving business. You can't get too dirty for Him to clean you. You can't drift too far away for Him to find you. He is able to save you right where you are.

Prayer: Our Father which art in heaven, thank you for salvation. Thank you that you did not let me die in sin. Strengthen me to share your saving grace today with others who do not know you as Savior. Amen

Day 9

Romans 6:23: *For the wages of sin is death; but the gift of God is eternal life through Jesus Christ our Lord.*

There are two absolute truths recorded here. The first is that "The wages of sin is death." Sin <u>always</u> pays its servants. We must never forget that sin is a master, an evil one. To practice sin, to live in sin, to reject Jesus Christ, is death!

To live as though you do not need a Savior is death – not just physical death, but eternal death. It is unending separation of the soul from God. Eternal death (the second death) and the lake of fire are identical terms (Rev. 20:14).

"For the wages of sin is death, but the gift of God is eternal life through Jesus Christ our Lord." Sin is that which proves to be unlike the character of God. Sin is missing the mark. It is contempt for and violation of the law of God. We have two choices in this life: the "wages of sin," or "the gift of God."

The second absolute truth recorded in this verse is:

"But the gift of God is eternal life through Jesus Christ our Lord."

We cannot earn this gift. We are undeserving of this gift. Yet it is what God wants to give. This "gift" is *"eternal life through Jesus Christ our Lord."* He alone has made salvation possible.

Prayer: Father of the redeemed, thank you for your Son, Jesus Christ, who took our sins upon Him, died in our place on the cross, and was buried in a borrowed tomb. Thank you for raising Him on that third day morning!

> Jesus paid it all;
> all to Him I owe.

Amen

Day 10

Psalms 23:1: *The Lord is my Shepherd; I shall not want.*

One who relies on the Lord to supply temporal needs has discovered the greatest security life can offer. No bank, no insurance company, no government program can promise to supply all our needs.

Notice the Lord did not promise to supply our wants, our desires, but our needs. The Shepherd knows that our desires are not always what is best for us. He keeps us from self-destruction. He supplies our needs. "I shall not want."

The Psalmist learned this way of life at a tender age. For many years he experienced the care of the Shepherd. I testify as well that *"the Lord my Shepherd"* has never failed me. Because of who the Shepherd is, I put my trust in Him without doubt. He supplies my needs. The Shepherd is all powerful, everlasting, all knowing. He knows what I need before I ask.

"The Lord is my Shepherd" – this is a personal

relationship. He knows me, and I know Him. He is with me daily. He watches over me nightly. I shall not want for safety. *"He never slumbers or sleeps."*

Do you need a Shepherd? Let Him be your Shepherd today.

Prayer: O Lord, God, to know you is to trust you. To know you is to cease to worry. To know you is to be unafraid in this life – the greatest success one can claim. Amen

𝕯𝖆𝖞 11

Isaiah 40:28: *Hast thou not known? Hast thou not heard, that the everlasting God the Lord, the Creator of the ends of the earth, fainteth not, neither is weary? There is no searching of His understanding. He giveth power to the faint; and to them that have no might He increaseth strength.*

Man must acknowledge God's greatness. It cannot be denied forever. It cannot be argued, for long. It cannot be overlooked, when all is said and done. God is everlasting. That alone makes Him worthy of our praise.

He is our Creator. He fashioned this world, and each of us. No one is like Him – never has been and never shall be. He's God, the only true and living God. Isaiah 40:25 says, *"To whom then will ye liken me, or shall I be equal? Saith the Holy One."*

Nothing you dream up, nothing you build, nothing you discover, is comparable to God. We worship Him because of who He is and what He has done. He alone has made salvation possible, through His Son Jesus Christ. Worship Him for His greatness, and worship Him for His mercy. Just worship Him.

Prayer: O Lord God, to know you is to trust you. To know you is to cease to worry. To know you is the greatest success one can claim. Amen

𝔇𝔞𝔶 12

Isaiah 55:1: *Ho, ever one that thirsteth, come ye to the waters, and he that hath no money; come ye, buy and eat; yea, come, buy wine and milk without money and without price.*

Salvation is free. Redemption's price has been paid by another, man's redeemer, the Suffering Servant, Jesus Christ. Isaiah wrote concerning Jesus Christ more than six hundred years before His birth in Bethlehem, *"Every one that thirsteth, come ye to the waters."*

Salvation is for all – Jews and Gentiles alike. The invitation is extended to all men. Romans 3:23 says, *"For all have sinned, and come short of the glory of God,"*

This is all-inclusive. It leaves no one out. Sin has infected the whole human race, but God has given us a way of escape through His Son Jesus Christ.

"Come ye to the waters," suggests there is a decision to be made. God makes an offer of eternal life, and it is free – not cheap, but free. Man's salvation cost

God the person of His Son Jesus Christ. Salvation is free. It is available. Yet man must accept it. Have you accepted it? Do you accept it right here, right now?

Share this gift with someone today! Tell someone about Jesus Christ! Tell them He died for our sin, and was raised for our justification. Tell them faith in Him saves from eternal ruin and doom. Tell them faith in Jesus Christ transforms us into eternal citizens. This is the saving faith. I trust Him as my Lord and Savior.

Prayer: Thank you, Lord God, for saving a sinner like me. Today and everyday, I will give you praise. Amen

𝔇𝔞𝔶 13

Psalms 24:1-2: *The earth is the Lord's and the fullness thereof; the world, and they that dwell therein. For He hath founded it upon the seas, and established it upon the floods.*

God is the Creator, the owner, the Sustainer of this universe in which we live. The phrase, *"they that dwell therein,"* includes us as well. Since God is the Creator of all things and the Sustainer of His creation, it is wise to acknowledge Him, and give thanks.

Is it healthy to begin each day and not acknowledge the Creator? There was a song a few years ago that said,

> I can't let a day go by
> without praising His name,
> I can't forget
> from whence I came.

How can we live well in this world without giving God thanks?

Prayer: Our Father, without you I am nothing. All that I am and all that I hope to be is by your grace. I am your servant! Amen

Day 14

Psalms 123:1-2: *Unto thee lift I mine eyes, O thou that dwellest in the heavens. Behold, as the eyes of servants look unto the hand of their masters, and as the eyes of a maiden unto the hand of her mistress; so our eyes wait upon the Lord our God, until that He have mercy upon us.*

How often do we look everywhere else than to God in our hour of need, only to discover there is no help without Him? We find no solution to our problems. Only then do we realize the upward look is the only one left.

He *that dwellest in the heavens* has all power in His hands. He alone directs the days and events of our lives. He knows where you are, and He knows what you are going through.

We must keep our eyes fixed on God, ready to obey His command, ready to move by faith. He will meet our every need. Nothing is impossible for the Lord our God. Biblical history is proof that He is an able God. He is our Defender, our Provider, and our All and All.

We can look to Him in our hour of need. He promised never to leave us alone. He is ever present. We are never alone.

Psalms 23:4 says, *"Yea, though I walk through the valley of the shadow of death, I will fear no evil; For thou are with me; thou rod and thou staff, they comfort me."*

In Matthew 28:20, Jesus says, *"Lo I am with you always, even to the end of the age."*

God knows all about us. He is aware of our daily activities. There is no need to worry.

Prayer: Our Father, without you I am nothing. All that I am and all that I hope to be is by your grace. I am your servant. O Lord, you know all about me. You know me better than I know myself. Amen

𝔇𝔞𝔶 15

Romans 8:1: *There is therefore now no condemnation to them which are in Christ Jesus, who walk not after the flesh, but after the Spirit.*

All are under condemnation without Christ. All have sinned and come short of the glory of God. Yet for those who trust Jesus Christ as their personal Savior, condemnation has been taken away.

Christ took the sins of the whole world upon Himself when He died on the cross. He took my place on the cross. He took your place. He paid the price for lost sinners.

Christ's suffering and death on the cross have taken condemnation away. He is our Savior, and He is able to save those who put their trust in Him. Trust Him, then! He will never reject those who put their trust in Him.

John 3:16 says, *"For God so loved the world, that He gave His only begotten Son, that whosoever believeth in Him should not perish, but have everlasting life."*

"Whosoever" is a wide word. It leaves no one out. Christ is the Savior of all who put their trust in Him.

Prayer: Gracious Father in heaven, I give you thanks for your Son Jesus Christ, who died for my sins, and was raised for my justification. The penalty has been taken away when I put my trust in Jesus Christ. Amen

𝕯𝖆𝖞 16

2 Corinthians 5:17: *Therefore if any man be in Christ, he is a new creature: old things are passed away; behold, all are become new.*

All that a believer receives in this world and in the world to come is "in Christ." Our eternal security is in Christ Jesus. Our assurance of salvation is in Christ Jesus.

This is the evidence: that God has given His Son to save lost sinners. According to John 3:16, God gave His Son that all who believe in Him can have eternal life. There is no other way to have life eternal.

"New Creature" describes someone divinely touched, someone transformed by the Spirit of God. It refers to regeneration, to new birth. As Ephesians 2:1-5 says:

> *"And you hath He quickened, who were dead in trespasses and sins; Wherein in time past ye walked according to the course of this world, according to the prince of the power of the air, the spirit that now worketh in the children of disobedience: Among whom also*

*we all had our conversation in times past in
The lust of our flesh, fulfilling the desires of
the flesh and of the mind; and were by nature
the children of wrath, even as others.*

*But God, who is rich in mercy, for His great
love wherewith He loved us, Even when we
were dead in sins, hath quickened us together
with Christ, (by grace ye are saved;)*

By His great love, we are made new, born of the
Spirit, born from above.

Prayer: Our Father in heaven, thank you for your
transforming power. Keep me, that I may live like a
child of God. Let my life be a witness for You.
Amen

𝔇𝔞𝔶 17

2 Corinthians 5:17: *Therefore if any man be in Christ, he is a new creature: old things are passed away; behold, all things are become new.*

Christ alone transforms sinners into saints. Christ alone brings us out of darkness into His marvelous light, by the regenerating work of the Holy Spirit. Christ alone is able to change sinful men.

Our trust is "in Christ," now and for eternity. Trust Him for salvation, physically, and spiritually! Christ not only saves to the uttermost, but He is able to provide for those who trust Him in this life.

The words *"if anyone"* mean, "yes, even such a one as me." Let this statement be yours today: 'I am one whom Christ has changed.' *"Old things are passed away."* By His grace, I have a brand new me.

Verse 18 says, *"And all things are of God, who has reconciled us to Himself by Jesus Christ, and hath given to us the ministry of reconciliation."*

As the old hymn says,

Jesus paid it all,
All to Him I owe,
Sin had left a crimson stain
He washed it white as snow.

Because of Christ I have a new life. Because of Him I have peace with God. Thank God for what He has done for me, so unworthy am I!

God has made a way through His Son for lost sinners. Today I give Him praise, glory, and honor. He is worthy of all our praises. Psalm 111:1 says, *"Praise ye the Lord, I will praise the Lord with my whole heart, in the assembly of the upright, and in the congregation."*

Prayer: Our Father in heaven, thank you for your transforming power. Keep me now, that I may live like a child of God. Let my life be a witness for You. I give you thanks. I give you praise for the great things you have done for me. Amen

𝕯𝖆𝖞 18

Romans 8:28: *And we know that all things work together for good to them that love God, to them who are the called according to His purpose.*

We may never understand how God can compute *"all things"* into good, but we must learn to trust Him. When circumstances seem unfavorable and problems impossible, let us remind ourselves that God is near, working on our behalf.

This is something God expects us to know. He is our Father and we are His children. He is doing what is best for us. His work in us and through us may be painful sometimes, but He knows what is best. He knows what it takes to make us like His Son Jesus Christ.

Whatever problems you may encounter today, know that God is near! He is here for you. Make sure you are here for Him as well.

God is always first. He is always to be praised. He is our Father, and He is our God. Again, we may never understand how God can compute *"all things"* into good. Some things are beyond our mind's understanding. Yet we can understand them in our souls, by faith. What we can do is trust Him in all circumstances.

Prayer: O God, today and everyday I trust you. I am not wise enough to understand life totally, but I trust that you know all things – past, present, and future. I trust that You have the power to take care of me. Amen

Day 19

Psalms 1:1-3: *Blessed is the man that walketh not in the counsel of the ungodly, nor standeth in the way of sinners, nor sitteth in the seat of the scornful. But his delight is in the law of the Lord; and in His law doth he mediate day and night. And he shall be like a tree planted by rivers of waters, that bringeth forth his fruit in his season; his leaf also shall not wither; and whatsoever he doeth shall prosper.*

This Psalm is a prescription for happiness. Take one three times a day, every day! First of all, "Blessed" means happy. The Psalmist is teaching us that happiness is not in things and stuff. Happiness is a lifestyle designed by God. He knows what is best for mankind. He made us. He knows His product.

A wise man once said that the happy man is marked as much by the things he does not do as by the things he does. He is marked by the places he does not go, the books he does not read, the movies he does not watch, the company he does not keep. We do well to keep that in mind every day.

The words 'walk', 'stand', and 'sit' in the Psalm

encompass a lifetime, and a lifestyle. *"Blessed is the man that walketh not in the counsel of the ungodly."*

Happiness is being fair, truthful, trustworthy. Happiness is building others up, not tearing them down.

"Blessed is the man who does not stand in the way of sinners." Happy is the one who does not participate in sinful activities with sinners, but is willing to point sinners to Christ.

"Blessed is the man who does not sit in the seat of the scornful." Happy is the one who avoids the seat of the scornful – their ideology, their man-made doctrine. The happy man is satisfied with the word of God. He delights in God's word.

What can truly make you happy today? Not things and stuff, not people and places! Happiness is to be born from above, to know Christ as Savior!.

Prayer: Our Father, teach me to say yes to Your will and Your way, that I may know true happiness! Create a lifestyle in me that will be pleasing to You. I want to be true. I want to be trustworthy. Amen

𝖣𝖆𝗒 20

Psalms 95:1-2: *O come, let us sing unto the Lord: let us make a joyful noise to the rock of our salvation.*

The Lord is worthy of a song, at worship and at home. He is worthy because of who He is, our Creator. He is our Sustainer, our Protector, and our Deliverer.

To know the Lord is a song, a song born in the heart. Sometimes the song needs only three words: "Thank you Lord." Sometimes it needs just two: "Praise Him." Sometimes one word is enough: "Alleluia."

A song does the soul good, and at the same time God is being praised. How can we be recipients of God's blessings and not have a song?

"Let us make a joyful noise to the rock of our salvation," because of who He is, and what He has done. He has made salvation available to all who will accept His Son as Savior. He has made us citizens of another world, where there is no more sickness, no more dying. He has given us an eternal home in glory.

Thank God for His grace and mercy!

Prayer: Thank you, God, for a song of thanksgiving and praise. You are worthy, O God, of our Alleluia. Salvation and glory and honor to the Lord our God! Amen

𝔇𝔞𝔶 21

Philippians 4:13: *I can do all things through Christ that strengtheneth me.*

Christ is my strength. I can do nothing without Him. Without Him, I will surely fail. I have come to understand my own frailty. I have come to grips with my own limitations.

Christ is my provider and my protector. I can depend on Him. He has never let me down. His strength is inexhaustible, and nothing is too hard for Him.

Life has its ups and downs, but Christ makes the difference. When the struggles of life come at you too fast and too hard, He gives you added strength to overcome.

Prayer builds your relationship with Him. Speak to Him, and listen for an answer. Through His word, the Bible, He will direct your life.

You are never alone. You are never helpless. To God be the glory, who is always there to meet our needs. As Psalm 27:1 says, *"The Lord is my light and my salvation; whom shall I fear? The Lord is the strength of my life; of whom shall I be afraid?"*

Prayer: Our Father, what a blessing it is to know that I am never alone! I know You are always here to direct my life. I know You are always here to protect and provide. I can do all things – even I – by Your grace and power. Amen

𝔇𝔞𝔶 22

Matthew 5:13-15: *Ye are the salt of the earth: but if the salt have lost his savour, wherewith shall it be salted? It is therefore good for nothing, but to be cast out, and to be trodden under foot of men. Ye are the light of the world. A city that is set on an hill cannot be hid. Neither do men light a candle, and put it under a bushel, but on a candlestick; and it giveth light unto all that are in the house.*

John MacArthur says one word can summarize these verses:"influence."   Salt and light are easily recognized wherever they are, because of their distinct qualities. Salt and light influence everything they touch. How does your life influence others?

With light comes life and knowledge. Christ is our light source. We have no light of our own. We are a reflection of Him.

Salt preserves from decay and gives flavor. His word in us is salt. He intends us to be salt – to be those who preserve and give flavor – in the world where we live.

Light and salt make this world a better place. Your light and salt should make your community, your workplace, your home a better place as well. Do they?

"Ye are the light of the world…Ye are the salt of the earth." You can make a difference. Shine, and bring out the best in others! Our society needs light and salt. In these dark times, when the world seems to be decaying, do something positive, something good! Influence your portion of the world for Jesus Christ!

Prayer: Gracious Father in heaven, help me today to be all that You would have me be. My desire is to touch those around me with the same love you lavished upon me. Amen

𝔇𝔞𝔶 23

Isaiah 55:1: *Ho, every one that thirsteth, come ye to the waters, and he that hath no money; come ye, buy, and eat; yea, come, buy wine and milk without money and without price.*

Three times in this verse God says "Come." This is an invitation to salvation – always free, but never cheap. God gave His only begotten Son that you and I might have eternal life. God gave His Son that sinners might be saved. Now He says to people from every nation "Come!"

Eternal life is free. What wonderful good news that is – because we ourselves are poverty-stricken. We have nothing to offer, no purchasing power. Knowing our condition, God makes salvation free.

Isaiah 55:2 says, *"Wherefore do ye spend money for that which is not bread? And your labour for that which satisfieth not? Harken diligently unto me, and eat ye that which is good, and let your soul delight itself in fatness."*

Many of us work long hard hours for worldly stuff:

new cars, a larger home, great vacations. All these things are temporal. God offers what is eternal. God offers eternal joy. Why are we satisfied with stuff that brings only a moment of happiness?

God has joy and nourishment that this world can never offer. Will you accept the invitation God has provided for mankind? If you are saved, if you are a born-again believer, share this invitation with a sinner!

Prayer: Our Father in heaven, thank you for salvation. Thank you for your Son Jesus Christ. His death, burial, and resurrection made salvation possible. Thank you that faith in your Son Jesus the Christ can save a sinner today. Amen

Day 24

Ephesians 2:8-9: *For by grace are ye saved through faith; and that not of yourselves: it is the gift of God: Not of works, lest any man should boast.*

The question modern minds often ask is, 'Saved from what?' We are saved from the penalty of sin.

Genesis 2:17 says, *"For in the day thou eatest thereof thou shalt surely die."* Adam and Eve died spiritually and began dying physically when they disobeyed God in the Garden of Eden. Spiritually they were separated from God. Physically, their bodies began to age and die.

Romans 5:12 tells us, *"Wherefore, as by one man sin entered into the world, and death by sin; and so death passed upon all men for that all have sinned."*

The first sin brought ruin to the human race. Adam's sin was imputed to his posterity. Every human being was in the loins of Adam when he transgressed, according to Romans 5:12-14. The penalties on the sons and daughters of Adam are: (1) physical death, (2) spiritual death, and (3) the second death (see

Revelation 20:6).

The penalty for sin is great, but it is not greater than the grace that saves. God has not left us without hope. Romans 6:23 says, *"For the wages of sin is death: but the gift of God is eternal life."*

Lewis Sperry Chafer wrote that, "Grace is what God may be free to do and indeed what He does accordingly for the lost, after Christ has died on behalf of them."

Prayer: Our Father in heaven, thank you for salvation. Thank you for your Son Jesus Christ. His death, burial, and resurrection make salvation possible. Faith in your Son Jesus the Christ can save a sinner today.

> Jesus paid it all.
> All to Him I owe.

Thank you, God, for Jesus. Amen

𝔇𝔞𝔶 25

Psalms 90:12: *So teach us to number our days, that we may apply our hearts unto wisdom.*

God is always God. He has been faithful. He has never failed man. We have seen His power, and to some degree we understand. As Psalm 90:1 says, *"Lord thou hast been our dwelling place in all generations."*

God is so tremendous that He knows! He is aware of all that has transpired, that is transpiring, and that will transpire. A *"dwelling place"* is a place of comfort and safety.

God is all-powerful, yet in His arms we too can feel secure. Therefore, we call on Him to teach us to number our days, because we understand tomorrow is not promised. We are not here to stay. We are moving toward a still unseen eternity.

Wisdom makes the right decisions at the right time. Wisdom plans for the future. Wisdom touches lives in a positive way. A heart saturated with wisdom will accept Christ as Savior, and live for Him. Wisdom teaches us that there is life daily beyond these mundane shores.

We are to live each day as though it is our last. Let us never forget our destiny is eternity, where there is no more sickness, no more dying. To trust Christ as Savior is to have eternal life. Jesus said in John 14: 6, *"I am the way, the truth, and the life: no cometh unto the Father but by me."*

Thank God for His Son Jesus Christ!

Prayer: Lord God, I can only say thank you. Open my eyes that I might see, and my ears that I might hear. Touch my heart that I may truly learn to love. Amen

𝕯𝖆𝖞 26

Matthew 7:1-2: *Judge not, that ye be not judged. For with what judgment ye judge, ye shall be judged: and with what measure ye mete, it shall be measure to you again.*

Unrighteous and unmerciful judgment is forbidden, because we do not have the final word. To judge another person's motives or to condemn them is to play God. How dangerous it is to play God! It is taking far too much on self.

In Romans 14:4, Paul asked, *"Who are you to judge the servant of another? To his own master he stands or falls."* The only one who has a right to judge any of us is the Lord. Though we cannot and we must not agree to false doctrine or unscriptural standards, we are never to judge a person's ministry, teaching, life, or motives by the standards we have set up.

God will judge us with the same judgment we use to judge others. If you have not been patient with others, do you expect God to be patient with you? We sometimes forget that God loves others just as much as He loves us – even those we think of as our enemies!

Prayer: Lord God, I can only say thank you. Open my eyes that I might see, and my ears that I might hear. Touch my heart that I may truly learn to love. Amen

Day 27

Galatians 6:7: *Be not deceived; God is not mocked: for whatsoever a man soweth, that shall he also reap.*

Don't be misled. You cannot live according to your every lust and expect God's blessings. There is a divine law. Sow evil, reap evil. Live to satisfy self and self only, and that's what you will reap.

There is a saying where I grew up: "What goes around comes around." Reaping what we first sow is a divine law. It is often ignored, yet we are not exempt from its consequences.

There are only two fields to sow in: the flesh, or the Spirit. Those who sow to the Spirit shall reap everlasting life. And those who sow to the flesh shall reap corruption.

God is the Creator of heaven and earth. He is the Giver and Sustainer of life. We are to live in such a way that God will be pleased with our lives, and that He will be glorified in us.

Who can tell if perhaps He will send good things our

way. *"He is the giver of every good and perfect gift."* Just remember: you reap what you sow. If you plant corn, do not expect to reap peas.

In the word of God, we are taught how to sow to the Spirit. Galatians 5:16 says, *"This I say then, Walk in the Spirit, and ye shall not fulfill the lust of the flesh."*

We are summoned to be Spirit-controlled, not to yield to the flesh.

Prayer: Our Father, thank you for an understanding of how life should be lived. You promised that if we plant a good crop, we will reap the good that we planted. Lord, I thank you for a plan, a guide to live by. Amen

𝖉𝖆𝖞 28

I Corinthians 13:1-3: *Though I speak with the tongues of men and of angels, and have not charity, I am become as sounding brass, or tinkling cymbal. And though I have the gift of prophecy, and understand all mysteries, and all knowledge; and though I have all faith, so that I can remove mountains, and have not charity, I am nothing. And though I bestow all my goods to feed the poor, and I give my body to be burned, and have not charity, it profiteth me nothing.*

In these three verses, the importance of "charity" is stressed. Charity is love. No gift, no action is complete in the absence of charity.

No matter how eloquent your speaking, if love is not the motivating factor, your words are only noise. I may have great faith, yet in the absence of charity, I am nothing.

Genuine love is of God. Love molds us into what God would have us be: people who love our neighbor, and even manage to love our enemies. Our world is in desperate need of love.

This day, I will ask God to help me to be more loving than I have been in the past.

Prayer: Gracious Father in heaven, the more I learn of Your love, the more I can truly love. I pray that all that I do will be motivated by love. Amen

𝔇𝔞𝔶 29

I Corinthians 13:13: *And now abideth faith, hope, charity, these three; but the greatest of these is charity (love).*

Divine love (agape) is everlasting. It is the God-like virtue. Impossible to define or totally explain, it can only be experienced.

John 3:16 says, *"For God so loved the world that He gave His only begotten Son, that whosoever believeth in Him should not perish, but have everlasting life."*

God loved us when we did not care for Him. He made provision for us when we could not help ourselves. We are summoned to love others, just as God has loved us.

He loved us so much that He gave His only begotten Son. God expressed His love to the world through giving His Son. What will you give today to God in return? What will you give others?

We can never repay God for what He has done. Even so, let what I give in response to His love be me – my mind, my heart, my hands, my feet! I surrender me.

Prayer: Our Father, thank you that I don't have to live foolishly. You supply the wisdom I need from day to day. Teach me to touch the lives of those around me with Your love! To You be glory, honor and praise. Amen

𝔇𝔞𝔶 30

Proverbs 9:1-6: *Wisdom hath builded her house, she hath hewn out seven pillars: She hath killed her beasts; she hath mingled her wine; she hath also furnished her table. She hath sent forth her maidens: she crieth upon the highest places of the city, Whoso is simple, let him turn in hither: as for him that wanteth understanding, she saith to him, Come eat of my bread, and drink of my wine which I have mingled. Forsake the foolish, and live; and go in the way of understanding.*

There is much to learn in the house of wisdom. It is a place for those who are simple, those who lack understanding. Wisdom offers a way of life tested and proven to be a blessing to all.

John MacArthur wrote, "The significance of the seven pillars is to convey the sufficiency of this house as full in size and fit for a banquet."

He went on to say, "Wisdom's blessings include her house and her hospitality."

These verses give us a picture of a bountiful banquet,

to which all are invited. There is nothing exclusive about wisdom's invitation. If someone seeks wisdom, let him ask of God. His Word is His direction, and is all we need to live.

Prayer: Teach me wisdom, precious Lord, so I may glorify you in all I do! Amen

Notes:

About the Author

Rev. Louis Vern Alexander, Senior, is the first of six children born to Lorene and L. Z. Alexander. Born in Forney, Texas, on April 25, 1943, he is the father of six children and eight grandchildren. His marriage of 36 years is to Marlene Alexander. He was called to ministry in October, 1974, and served as Assistant Minister at Mt. Horeb Baptist Church, Waxahachie, Texas, from 1975 to 1981. Rev. Alexander was called as pastor of the St. Matthew Baptist Church in Dallas on February 7, 1981.

Pastor Alexander's extracurricular activities include:
- Moderator of the Friendship Baptist District Association – 2010 to present
- Member of the Steering Committee of the D. Edwin Johnson Theological Institute
- 1st Vice Moderator of the Friendship District Association
- Chaplain at Tri-City Hospital
- Board Member of Dallas Ser-Jobs for Progress, Inc.
- Teacher in the Friendship District Congress
- Member of the Friendship District Scholarship Board
- Member of the Oak Cliff Baptist Minister's Union

- Ministerial Advisor for OCBMU Ministers' Wives Ministry
- Member of the Skillful Living Center Program
- Member of the Dalworth Interdenominational Ministerial Alliance:
  > 1st Vice President from 1988 to 1990; Secretary from 1986 to 1987

Pastor Alexander's education includes:
- Tyndale Seminary, Ft. Worth, TX
  > 2001 to present
  > 1992-1995
- Southern Bible Institute, Dallas, TX
  > 1990-1991
  > 1977-1978
- Jarvis Christian College, Hawkins, TX
  > 1962-1963
- Dalworth High School, Grand Prairie, TX
  > 1953-1962

Also from Searchlight Press

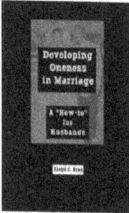

Developing Oneness in Marriage:
A 'How-to' for Husbands
by Rev. Dr. Lloyd C. Blue
(Searchlight Press, 2011)

Character Is Key:
In Sports and in Life
by Eddie Hill and Dr. Jim Moore
(Searchlight Press, 2010)

Headed the Wrong Direction?
Calling Us and Others
Back from the Edge
by Rev. Wade J. Simmons
(Searchlight Press, 2011)

Wonderworking Power:
A Fresh Translation
of the Gospel of Mark
by John Cunyus
(Searchlight Press, 2011)

Thirty Days to Overcoming, 69

The Way of Wisdom:
Job, Proverbs, Ecclesiastes,
Song of Solomon
by John Cunyus
(Searchlight Press, 2008)

The Audacity of Prayer:
A Fresh Translation of the Book of Psalms
by John Cunyus
(Searchlight Press, 2009)

The Latin Torah:
Genesis, Exodus, Leviticus, Numbers,
Deuteronomy
by John Cunyus
(Searchlight Press, 2010)

Searchlight Press
Who are you looking for?
Publishers of thoughtful Christian books since 1994.
5634 Ledgestone Drive
Dallas, TX 75214-2026
888.896.6081
info@Searchlight-Press.com
www.Searchlight-Press.com

www.ingramcontent.com/pod-product-compliance
Lightning Source LLC
Chambersburg PA
CBHW031612040426
42452CB00006B/482